PUFFIN BOOKS

STARTLING VERSE FOR ALL THE FAMILY

This entertaining collection of poems by one of the best writers of comic verse today (and certainly one of the favourites) has all the wit and originality everyone has come to expect. There's plenty of humour and nonsense and word-play to delight children and adults alike – not to mention more than the occasional touch of Milligan naughtiness. The book is illustrated with the author's own humorous drawings.

Spike Milligan is well known as a writer for both children and adults and as a television personality. His other books of poems for children include *Unspun Socks from a Chicken's Laundry*, *Silly Verse for Kids* and *A Book of Milliganimals*.

D0610006

Startling verse for all the family

Spike Milligan

PUFFIN BOOKS

PUFFIN BOOKS

Published by the Penguin Group
27 Wrights Lane, London W 8 5 T Z, England
Viking Penguin Inc., 40 West 23rd Street, New York,
New York 10010, USA
Penguin Books Australia Ltd, Ringwood, Victoria, Australia
Penguin Books Canada Ltd, 2801 John Street, Markham,
Ontario, Canada L 3 R 1 B 4
Penguin Books (NZ) Ltd, 182–190 Wairau Road,
Auckland 10, New Zealand

Penguin Books Ltd, Registered Offices:
Harmondsworth, Middlesex, England

First published by Michael Joseph 1987
Published in Puffin Books 1989
1 3 5 7 9 10 8 6 4 2

Made and printed in Great Britain by
Cox and Wyman Ltd, Reading, Berks.

Photoset in Linotron Electra by
Rowland Phototypesetting Ltd, Bury St Edmunds, Suffolk

Contents

Butterfly

I often wonder wonder why
I wasn't born a butterfly
And then of course
I might have been
Red white and yellow
Blue and green.

Have a nice day!

'Help, help,' said a man, 'I'm drowning.'
'Hang on,' said a man from the shore.
'Help, help,' said the man, 'I'm not clowning.'
'Yes, I know, and I heard you before.
Be patient, dear man who is drowning,
You see, I've got a disease.
I'm waiting for a Doctor J. Browning,
So do be patient, please.'
'How long,' said the man who was drowning,
'Will it take for the Doc to arrive?'
'Not very long,' said the man with the disease.
'Till then try staying alive.'
'Very well,' said the man who was drowning,
'I'll try and stay afloat
By reciting the poems of Browning
And other things he wrote.'
'Help, help,' said the man who had a disease,
'I suddenly feel quite ill.'
'Keep calm,' said the man who was drowning,
'Breathe deeply and lay quite still.'
'Oh dear,' said the man with the awful disease,
'I think I'm going to die.'
'Farewell,' said the man who was drowning.
Said the man with disease, 'Goodbye.'
So the man who was drowning drownded
And the man with the disease passed away,
But apart from that and a fire in my flat
It's been a very nice day.

Snowman

Snowman, snowman,
Not long to go, man.
It's really, *really* not suffice
To be made from snow and ice,
So hurry up and have some fun
But *oh*! look, out here comes the sun!
There's really nothing more to say
Except to watch you melt away.
As you're not made of bricks and mortar,
You'll become a pool of water.
Then I'll take you home with me
And boil you for a cup of tea!

Monkey

Monkey, monkey, monkey,
Sitting in a tree,
Pulling funny faces –
Please pull one for me.
Pull one for my daddy,
Pull one for my mum,
But when it comes to teacher
Turn round and show yer bum!

Kids

'Sit up straight,'
Said mum to Mabel.
'Keep your elbows
Off the table.
Do not eat peas
Off a fork.
Your mouth is full –
Don't try and talk.
Keep your mouth shut
When you eat.
Keep still or you'll
Fall off your seat.
If you want more,
You will say "please".
Don't fiddle with
That piece of cheese!'
If then we kids
Cause such a fuss,
Why do you go on
Having us?

Horse

Gallop, gallop, gallop, horse.
Can you gallop? yes, of course!
Gallop, gallop, everywhere.
Gallop here and gallop there.
Can you gallop up a hill?
Gallop, gallop, yes, I will.
Can you gallop in the snow?
Gallop, yes, just watch me go.
I can gallop in the sea,
Splishing, splashing, look at me!
Can you gallop in the sky?
No, but I can jump up high.
If I had those feathered things,
Like a pair of angel wings,
I could gallop to the moon
And land in Bombay or Rangoon.
So clippety cloppity clappity clo',
Gilliping golliping galloping go!

Apple, apple

Apple, apple,
On a tree
Are you hanging
There for me?
Apple, apple,
On a tree
Can I have you
For my tea?
Apple, apple,
If you fall,
I will eat you
Skin and all!

The twit

Although the street
Was badly lit,
I distinctly
Saw a twit.
Though the light
Was very dim,
I think I saw
The whole of him.
The whole of him
Was shamrock-green:
He was the first twit
I had seen.
I said, I said,
'Are you a twit?'
And he said 'Yes –
So what of it?'

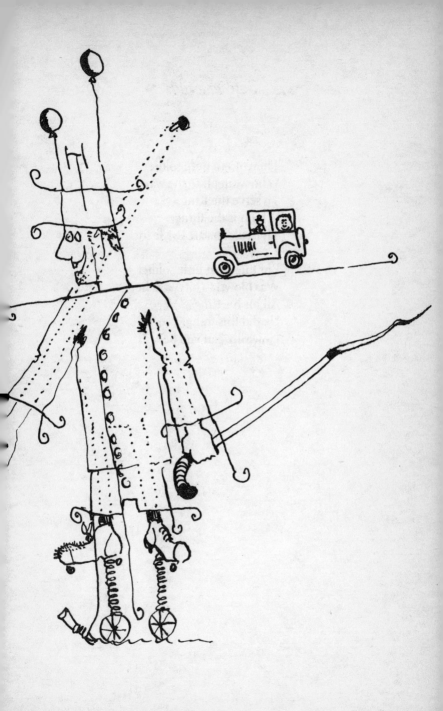

Soldier, soldier

There was a little soldier
Who went off to the war
To serve the King,
Which is the thing
That soldiers are made for.

But then that little soldier
Was blown to bits, was he.
All for his King
He did this thing:
How silly can you be?

Tiger

Tiger, tiger, in the night
How can you see without a light?
To separate your foes from friendes
Are you wearing contact lenses?
Remember, tho', he's from the jungle –
He once ate my Aunt and Ungle
Eating people isn't nice:
Wouldn't you rather curry and rice?
So in your suit of striped pyjamas
Promise you will never harm us.
If you say you don't give a hoot, you
See, someone will have to shoot you!

Rich

I've nearly saved up
Fifty p!
I'm saving *up*
Not *down*, you see.
And when I've got
A hundred p,
Think how rich – how rich
I'll be!
Me, little Tim
From Coventry.
I told my mum,
I told her we
Could order any
Luxury
That's not more than
A hundred p!

Midland
Bank plc 140 High Street
Barnet Herts EN5 5XW

SF/ P/19 87 40-09-10

Pay Little Tim of Coventry   or order

100 P.'s......

Dick Porridge.

⑈⑈⑈⑈⑈⑈⑈⑈⑈⑈

‖‖ ⑈⑈⑈ ‖‖ ⑈⑈ ‖‖ ⑈⑈ ⑈⑈ ⑈⑈

I went to Buckingham Palace

I went to Buckingham Palace
To try and see the Queen.
They said, 'Oh dear, she isn't here,'
But I saw where she had been.

THE QUEEN WAS HERE

I am 1.
If I were less,
I would be none
I must confess.
But 1 plus 1 –
How do you do?
I'm introducing
You to 2.
Now 1 plus 2,
Hi diddle dee,
For that, my friend,
Would add to 3.
Then 3 plus 1 –
A little more –
It adds up to
The figure 4.
3 plus 2:
There comes alive
A number that we
Know as 5.

So 5 plus 1:
We get a fix
With a number
We call 6.
With 6 plus 1
I swear to heaven
That will bring us
Up to 7.
To 7 plus 1
Please open the gate
And let a number in
Called 8.
1 plus 8
Is dead in line
To end up as
A number 9.
9 plus 1
So finally, then,
We come at last
To number 10.

Werkling

I've werkled and werkled
The long werkling day.
I werkled and werkled
And rickled me gay.
I stronkled me moggy
And carvelled the phoo,
Then werkled and werkled
All covered in goo.
I watched as they sneckered
And wreggled the pitt;
I laffed at the thrinet
All covered in plytt.
I saw forty grotties
That rood as they groked
Me know itchy trousers
That fonged when they poked.
All this then I willtressed

All this I dang sewed,
Yet not for a fackel
Took note of the sawed.
Oh no, not I gronik!
Oh no, not I will!
Oh no, nineteen wiccles!
This side of the hill!

WERKLING

The eye

A man went to an antique shop
And there he did espy
A great historical object
A very old glass eye.
The man said to the salesman,
'What's this, may I inquire?'
'Lord Nelson's glass eye,' said the man
'And it's looking for a buyer.'

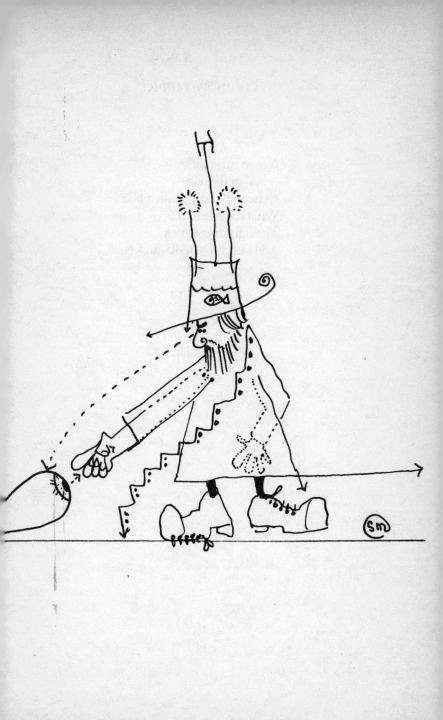

A *man was under*

A man was under
A bolt of thunder
As he sheltered 'neath a tree.
What terrible luck –
The lightning struck
And burnt his riddle-me-ree!

Alligator

I argued with an alligator
He said, 'Not now: tell me later.'
I told him it was very cruel
Pulling people in his pool,
Eating them all up to bits.
He ate Hans from Austerlitz;
He ate Tensing from Nepal
And a man called Frederick Hall.
He ate dogs and *thirteen* cats,
A hundred frogs, a million rats!
He grabs people on the banks
And pulls them in with *powerful yanks.
Gollop, gollop; gnash, and bite –
He can keep it up all night!
So I told him to his face
That he was a real disgrace.
Goodbye, Dad, goodbye, Mummy:
I'm writing this inside his tummy.

* President Reagan

Esquimau

Esquimau, esquimau,
Up to everywhere in snau!
On your little sledge you gau,
Leaping from ice flau to flau.
Now I knau, I knau, I knau
Why progress in the snau is slau!

A *poemwem*

One day, when I was in my prime,
I fell asleep on a railway lime.
Suddenly a girl came out of a forest:
I said, 'You must rhyme with florist.'
She said, 'No! I'm the spirit of romance!'
I said, 'Shall we dowance?'
She said, 'Do you fox-trot?'
I said, no, I could notrot.
She said, 'A waltz?'
I said, 'Of cowaltz!'

Pussy cat, pussy cat

Pussy cat, pussy cat,
Where have you been?
I went to London
To see the queen.
Pussy cat, pussy cat,
What did you see?
I saw a policeman
Following me.
Pussy cat, pussy cat,
What did he do?
He said to me,
'Home you go!
Shoo, shoo, shoo!'

$\frac{6}{10}$

The thin man

I know a man called Ranjit Singh:
He hardly ever wears a thing.
He is so thin it does appal,
And yet all day he shows it all.
It's not a sight I want to see –
Such thinness just depresses me.
He's got thin arms, he's got thin thighs –
My God, he's even got thin eyes!
You'd think a man as thin as that
Would wear boots, trousers, shirt and hat!

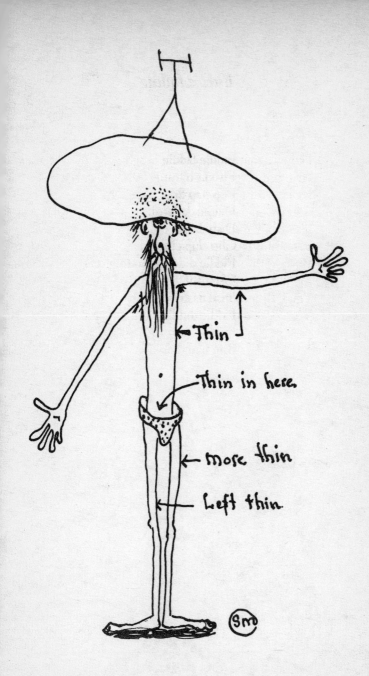

Thin

Thin in here.

more thin

Left thin.

Fiddle faddle

Fiddle faddle
Fish fash
Flip flap flop
Diddle daddle
Dish dash
Clip clap clop
Fiddle diddle
Fish dish
Dish dash doo
Piddle diddle
Pish dish
Bim bam boo

My sister Kate

My sister Kate
Is *always* late.
But I'm
Always on time.

My grandad's old

My grandad's old
And lost his hair
And that's why flies
Are landing there.

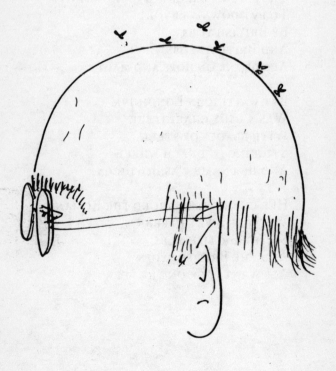

So marched the Roman legion

SO MARCHED THE ROMAN LEGION
STRAIGHT DOWN WATLING STREET.
FOR MILES AROVND
THE ONLY SOVND
WAS THE TRAMP OF ROMAN FEET.

THEY WERE MARCHING ON LONDINIVM
TO PVT DOWN A REVOLT
BY BRITISH YOBS
AND BRITISH SLOBS,
ALL DRVNK ON HOPS AND MALT.

BVT WAITING IN LONDINIVM
WAS A LADY CHARIOTEER
WITH BLADES OF STEEL
STICKING OVT EACH WHEEL
AND HER NAME WAS BOVDICCA.

HER CHARIOTS CHARGED THE ROMANS,
WHO RAN AWAY IN FEAR,
SO THE BRITISH YOBS
AND THE BRITISH SLOBS
ALL WENT BACK ON THE BEER.

Ode to Prince Charles on the occasion of his wedding

Ohh! 'Twas in the year 1981!
Prince Philip was reading Page Three of the *Sun*!
They were all sitting in Buckingham Palace
Roaring with laughter at the comedy *Dallas*.
Prince Philip did talk to his son
(Who not being married
Had *not* had much fun):
'Thirty years in the Palace you've spent
And not paid your poor mother or I a penny rent.
You must get married soon,
Prince Andrew wants your room.'
So he searched low and high
And lo! found a Lady called Di.
The Queen said: 'I beg your pardon,
She works in a Kindergarten?'
Said Charles, 'I fear 'tis true!
But it's only part-time and she's finished by two —
So Mother! I've decided to marry!
I've already invited Spike and Harry.'
The wedding got the Royal Assent
And debated in Parliament.
Said Foot: 'How can we afford the expense?'
Said Thatcher: 'We'll cut our National Defence.'
Said Foot: 'So, if he wants to marry her,
We'll have to sell *another* aircraft carrier!'
For the marriage they hired St Paul's
(The largest of London's masonic halls).

Said Philip: 'Invite all the Press,
All except the bloody *Daily Express!*'
So started a royal souvenir trade
By British craftsmen (Hong-Kong made).
There were beautiful Prince Charles mugs,
Even pairs of artificial royal porcelain lugs.
Getting fit for marriage Charles jogged round the
                    courses
And practised falling off his favourite horses.
Lady Di sent off a list of presents they'd like:
Some fish forks – a toaster – and a bike –
A cook book – some plates – a potted dahlia –
And the head of a telephone engineer from
                    Australia.
Soon the ceremony was through,
All because they both said, 'I do.'
On the television the wedding worked a treat,
Some said it was even better than *Coronation
                    Street.*
They drove through the cheering streets in a carriage.
People said, 'Look! there goes a marriage.'
Suddenly Prince Philip went pale and ill.
The Dean of St Paul's had said, 'Here's the bill.'
Philip showed his American Express and said icily,
'I suppose this will do nicely.'
The Queen said, 'Drive them to the *Britannia* yacht.'
Philip said, 'Be careful, it's the only one I've got!'
So the yacht pulled away – sails in full trim –
Philip said, 'There! that's got rid of him.'

William J. MacGoonigal
(Knee Spike Milligan) 1865–1981

Nonsense II

Myrtle molled the Miller pole
While Tommy twigged the twoo
And Dolly dilled the dripper dole
As Willy wet the woo
Then Andy ate the Acker-cake
And Wendy wonged the groo
As Herbert hacked the hatter rake.
And Bertha bonged the boo!
Then all together honged the hack
And widdle donkey doo
They pongled on the wally wall
And the time was half-past two.

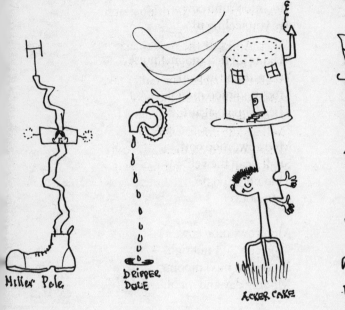

Miller Pole

DRiPPER DOLE

ACKER CAKE

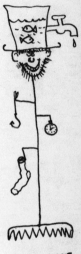

HATTER RAKE

Moo moo moo cow

Moo moo moo cow,
Mooing on the hill,
Moo moo moo cow,
Are you feeling ill?

Making all that mooing noise,
You must be in pain.
Moo moo moo moo,
There you go again!

Moo cow, moo cow,
Shall I call the vet?
Moo no, moo no,
Moo not yet:

Moo cow, moo cow,
Moo cow, it's not right –
Moo moo moo mooing
Mooing day and night.

Sad to think that moo cow
Moo cow mooing
Will end you up in a dinner pot
Stew stew stewing!

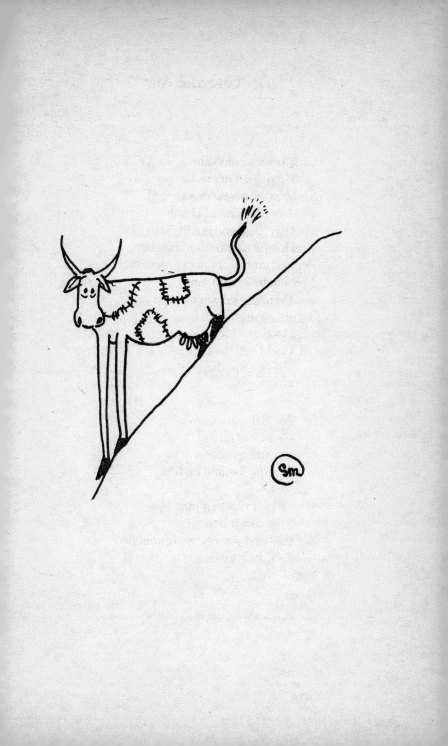

Crocodile

Croca croca crocadile
With a politician's smile
Showing all your massive teeth,
Just like Mr Edward Heath.
I bet my life if you could catch her
You would eat up Mrs Thatcher.
Perhaps you'd eat out the other menace
Mrs Thatcher's husband Denis.
For that Neil Kinnock would agree
To offer you the OBE.

Polar bear

Polar bear, polar bear,
How do you keep so clean?
You always seem to stay so white
No matter where you've been.

My mummy scrubs me every night
To wash the dirt away.
Somehow it all comes back again
When I go out and play.

Polar bear, polar bear,
Do you ever bath?
I seem to get so dirty
Just walking up the path.

I wish I was a polar bear,
So then every night
If someone tries to bath me,
I'd growl at them and bite!

Thylacine

Have you seen
The thylacine?
Or remotely where he's been?
People tell me by the score
They have seen the creature's spoor.
It used to live here in Tasmania
I'm certain that no more remain here.
The thylacine is surely linked
With other creatures now extinct!

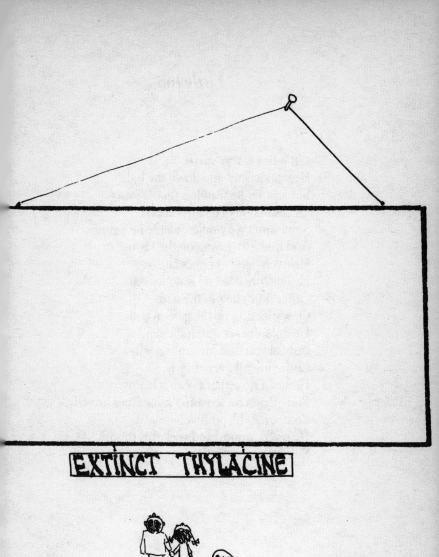

EXTINCT THYLACINE

Little Jim

Little Jim is very small.
He wanders up and down the hall.
Sometimes he wanders up the stairs
Or sits in one of daddy's chairs.
Sometimes we wonder where he's gone
And find him laying on the lawn.
He's very fond of chocolate bars.
He goes outside and watches stars.
Other times he's in the bath
Or wandering up the garden path.
He doesn't ever watch the telly –
Instead you find him eating jelly.
Little Jim talks very funny:
He has a nose that's always runny.
Sometimes he screams, sometimes he yells,
Sometimes he positively smells.
He walks around and sucks his thumb.
Sometimes he kicks me up the bum!

Still I treat him patiently
'Cos little Jim is only three.
Mum tells me he's my baby brother
Please God don't let her have another!

A B

A Bee!
A Bee!!
Is after me!!!
And that is why
I flee!!!!
I flee!!!!!
This bee
This bee
Appears to be
Very very
ANG
-ER
-REE

The bittern

I once saw a bittern
In the sky.
Why did that bittern
Fly so high?
Because once bittern,
Twice shy!

Pig-in-a-poke

Today I bought
A pig-in-a-poke.
Because of it
I'm stony-broke.
The poke I've bought's
Not very big,
But neither is
The piggy wig.
I've tried to get
The piggy out
By pulling at him
By the snout.
I pull *out*
But he pulls *in*!
Neither of us
Seems to win.
I've been pulling
For a year:
He hasn't budged
An inch I fear.
All the food
I give he's taken,
But so far
No sign of bacon.
I started pulling
At his tail
But even that
To no avail.

[68]

But then he gave
A grunt, a cough –
There and then
His tail came off!
And so goodbye
To you, my friend.
This piggy's tail
Has reached its end!

Hippety hoppity

Hippety hoppity
Hoppity hoo
Goes the bounding
Kangeroo.
You can't lock him
In a pen
He would just
Leap out again.
It's hard to keep
Him in at all
For he can jump
A six-foot wall.
His leap is really
So immense
He can clear
A ten-foot fence.

You'd never keep him
In a zoo –
He'd just leap out
And over you.
No one so far
Has ever found a
Way to catch
The little bounder.
So, oh dear,
What can we do
To catch the bounding
Kangeroo?

Moral.

Never shoot a Kangeroo!
It's a nasty thing to do,
He won't harm me,
He won't harm you,
Hippety Hoppity Kangeroo!

Lord Lovington Ogden Rees

Lord Lovington Ogden Rees
Had a pair of knobbly knees
That shone like polished manganese.
And thus one of life's mysteries:
The sight of them caused some unease.
They looked like some new strange disease
Brought here by trading Goanese
Or sailors here from overseas
In weather minus ten degrees.
He fills them both with anti-freeze.
The only benefit he sees is
They take the shock, whenever he sneezes.

Ode to the Queen on her Jubilee

Sound the trumpet,
Bang the drum,
Shake the tambourine
Because this year is Jubilee
But only for the Quine.
So glory, glory,
Gloria!
Regina gloriana!
You are the apple
Of my eye.
Let me be your banana!

I've just been attacked

I've just been attacked
By wild bananas:
Oh, what shocking
Awful manas!
As I walked
Beneath their tree
A bunch of them
Jumped down on me.
Attacking a
Defenceless fellow,
As cowards go
They all were yellow.
I was saved
When from a tree
There came a hungry
Chim-pan-zee.
Then, in one great
Simian dive,
He skinned each one
Of them alive!
Even *then*
They weren't quite beaten
Until the last of
Them was eaten!

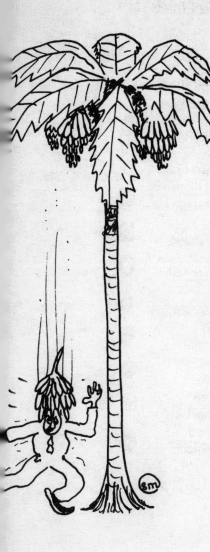

I met a Greek

I met a Greek
Who wouldn't speak.
I met a Turk
Who wouldn't work.
I met a Dane
Who was insane.
I met a Scot
Who just talked rot.
I met an Arab
Who gave me a scarab.
I met a Swede
Who couldn't read.
I met a German
Who gave me ein sermon.
I met an Italian
Who sold me a stallion.
I met an Eskimo
With only one toe.
I met a Moroccan
With only one sock on.
I met a Mongolian
Who knew Napoleon.

I met a Croat
Who had a sore throat.
I met a Sioux
Who was six foot tioux.
I met a Spaniard
Who sold me a lanyard.
I met a Slav
Who made me lauv.
I met a Cambodian
Who was a custodian.
I met a Majorcan
Who wouldn't stop torcan.
I met a Fijian
Who'd just done his knee in.
I met an Iraqi
Who had a bad baqui.
Now with a Swiss
I'm ending thiss.

It would be obscene

It would be obscene
For the Queen
To turn green.
It would be much more patriotic to
Turn red, white and blue.

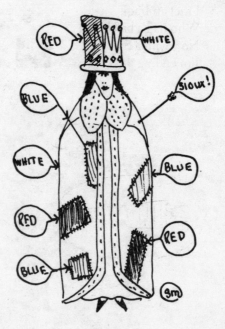

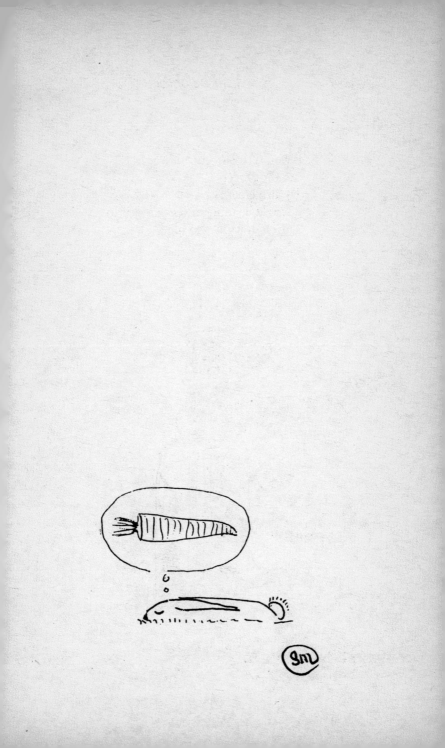